Animals

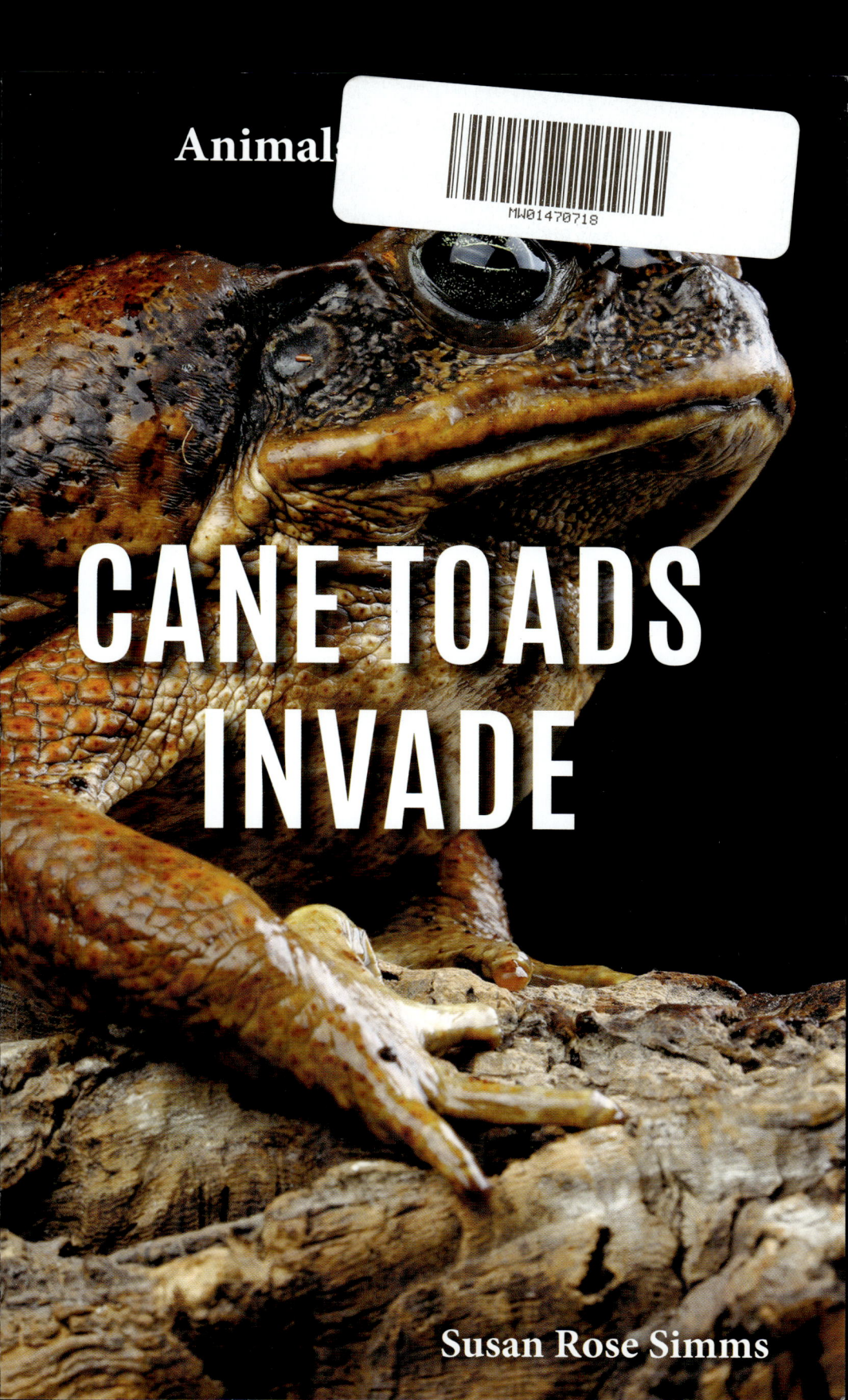

CANE TOADS INVADE

Susan Rose Simms

WWW.APEXEDITIONS.COM

Copyright © 2025 by Apex Editions, Mendota Heights, MN 55120. All rights reserved. No part of this book may be reproduced or utilized in any form or by any means without written permission from the publisher.

Apex is distributed by North Star Editions:
sales@northstareditions.com | 888-417-0195

Produced for Apex by Red Line Editorial.

Photographs ©: Shutterstock Images, cover, 1, 4–5, 12–13, 14–15, 16–17, 18–19, 20–21, 24–25, 28–29, 30–31, 32–33, 34–35, 40–41, 44–45, 48–49, 50–51, 52–53, 54–55, 56–57; Brian Cassey/AP Images, 6–7; iStockphoto, 8–9, 27, 36–37; imageBroker/Emanuele Biggi/Newscom, 10–11; Queensland Department of Environment and Science/AP Images, 22–23; Joe Raedle/Getty Images News/Getty Images, 39; Kaoru Tachibana/Yomiuri Shimbun/AP Images, 42–43; Sui Chou/AFP/Getty Images, 46–47; Red Line Editorial, 58–59

Library of Congress Control Number: 2023922205

ISBN
979-8-89250-209-2 (hardcover)
979-8-89250-230-6 (paperback)
979-8-89250-271-9 (ebook pdf)
979-8-89250-251-1 (hosted ebook)

Printed in the United States of America
Mankato, MN
082024

NOTE TO PARENTS AND EDUCATORS

Apex books are designed to build literacy skills in striving readers. Exciting, high-interest content attracts and holds readers' attention. The text is carefully leveled to allow students to achieve success quickly.

TABLE OF CONTENTS

Chapter 1
TOAD BUSTING 4

Chapter 2
A BIG PROBLEM 8

Chapter 3
TOADS IN AUSTRALIA 17

That's Wild!
CLOSE CALL 26

Chapter 4
TOADS IN FLORIDA 28

That's Wild!
THE TOAD BUSINESS 38

Chapter 5
AROUND THE WORLD 40

Chapter 6
MANAGING CANE TOADS 50

MAP • 58
COMPREHENSION QUESTIONS • 60
GLOSSARY • 62
TO LEARN MORE • 63
ABOUT THE AUTHOR • 63
INDEX • 64

Chapter 1
TOAD BUSTING

One morning in Australia, people step outside to a surprise. No people are on the street. But the street isn't empty. It's filled with thousands of cane toads.

People often catch cane toads after the sun sets. The toads are typically active at night.

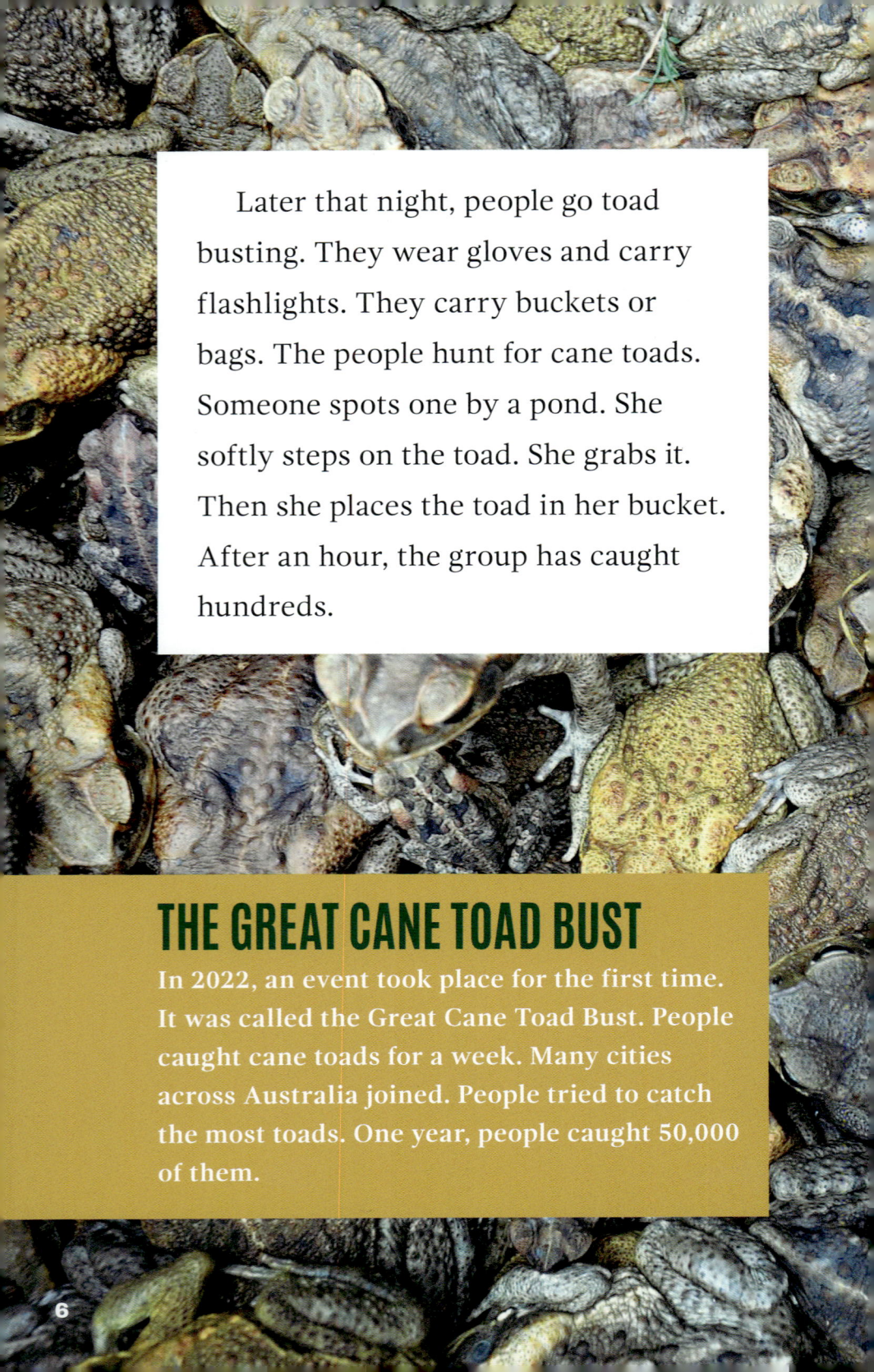

Later that night, people go toad busting. They wear gloves and carry flashlights. They carry buckets or bags. The people hunt for cane toads. Someone spots one by a pond. She softly steps on the toad. She grabs it. Then she places the toad in her bucket. After an hour, the group has caught hundreds.

THE GREAT CANE TOAD BUST

In 2022, an event took place for the first time. It was called the Great Cane Toad Bust. People caught cane toads for a week. Many cities across Australia joined. People tried to catch the most toads. One year, people caught 50,000 of them.

One cane toad bust event in Australia happens every March. It is called "Toad Day Out."

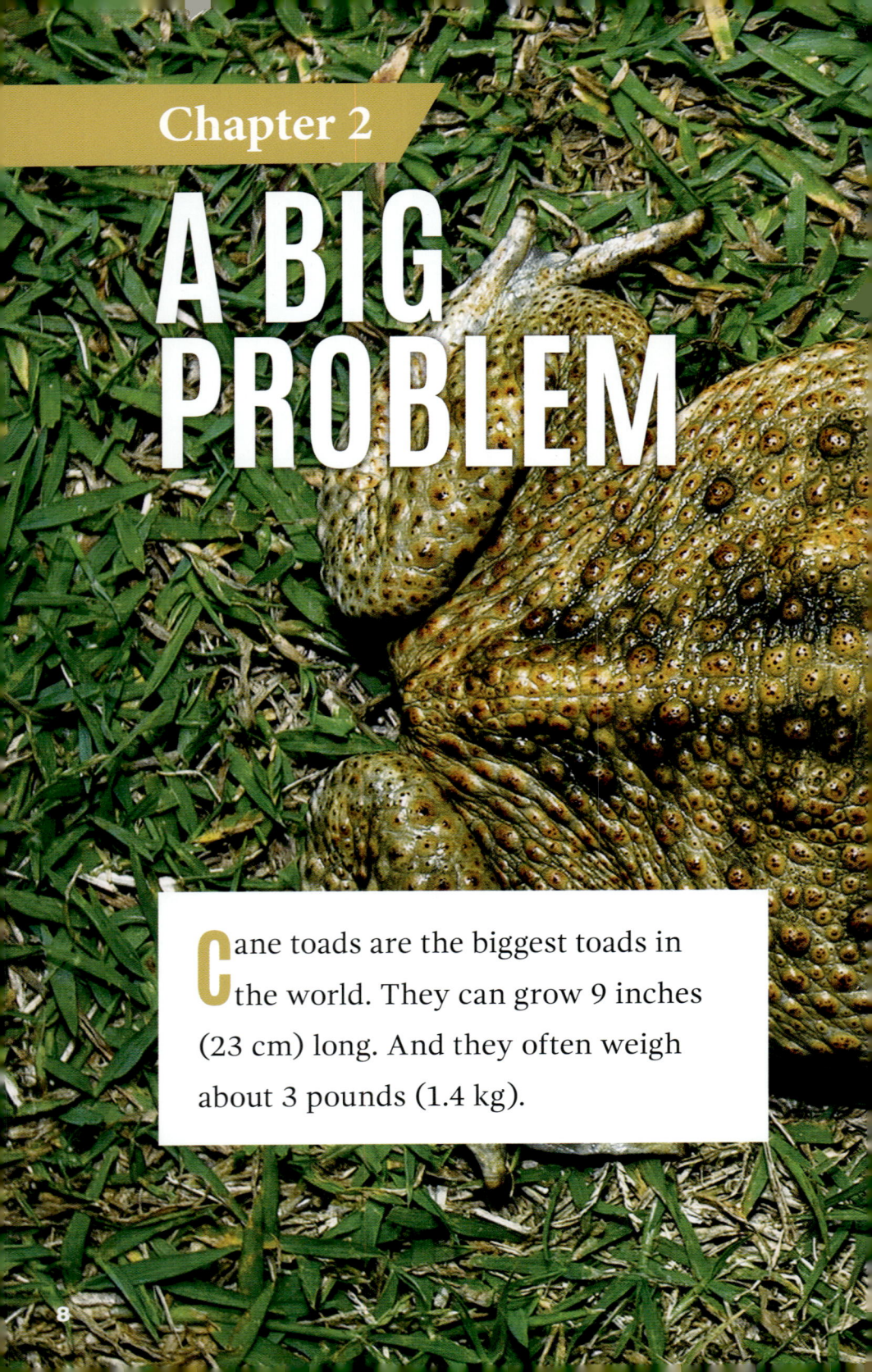

Chapter 2
A BIG PROBLEM

Cane toads are the biggest toads in the world. They can grow 9 inches (23 cm) long. And they often weigh about 3 pounds (1.4 kg).

Female cane toads are typically bigger than males.

A cane toad's poison looks milky white.

The cane toad's size helps it survive. Its poison helps, too. Each toad has glands on its shoulders. These glands hold poison. They release it if the toad feels scared or threatened. This poison is strong. It can kill many kinds of animals.

ALWAYS TOXIC

Cane toad eggs are poisonous. So are the tadpoles. Young toads are less toxic. But they start growing their poisonous glands. As a result, the toads become more poisonous as they age.

Cane toads are native to the Americas. They've been common in South and Central America for many years. However, colonists brought the toads to new places. In the 1800s, they introduced sugarcane to the Caribbean. They started sugarcane farms throughout the region. Native beetles started killing sugar crops there. So, colonists brought cane toads. They hoped the toads would eat the beetles.

Beetles ate the roots of sugarcane plants. Greyback cane beetles were one type of these beetles.

13

In the 1930s, people brought cane toads to other places. Hawai'i and Australia were two examples. People hoped the toads would eat beetles. Instead, the toads spread very quickly. Soon, some areas had millions of toads. They became one of the worst invasive species in the world.

NO PREDATORS IN NEW PLACES

In their native homes, cane toads have predators. Some animals can eat the toads without getting sick. Others know to avoid the poisonous parts. But in new places, cane toads may not have predators. Or they may kill animals that eat them. As a result, the toads spread quickly.

Some Australian animals, such as kookaburras, can survive eating cane toads.

15

The Kimberley has many waterfalls and rivers. It's also known for its steep cliffs and sandy beaches.

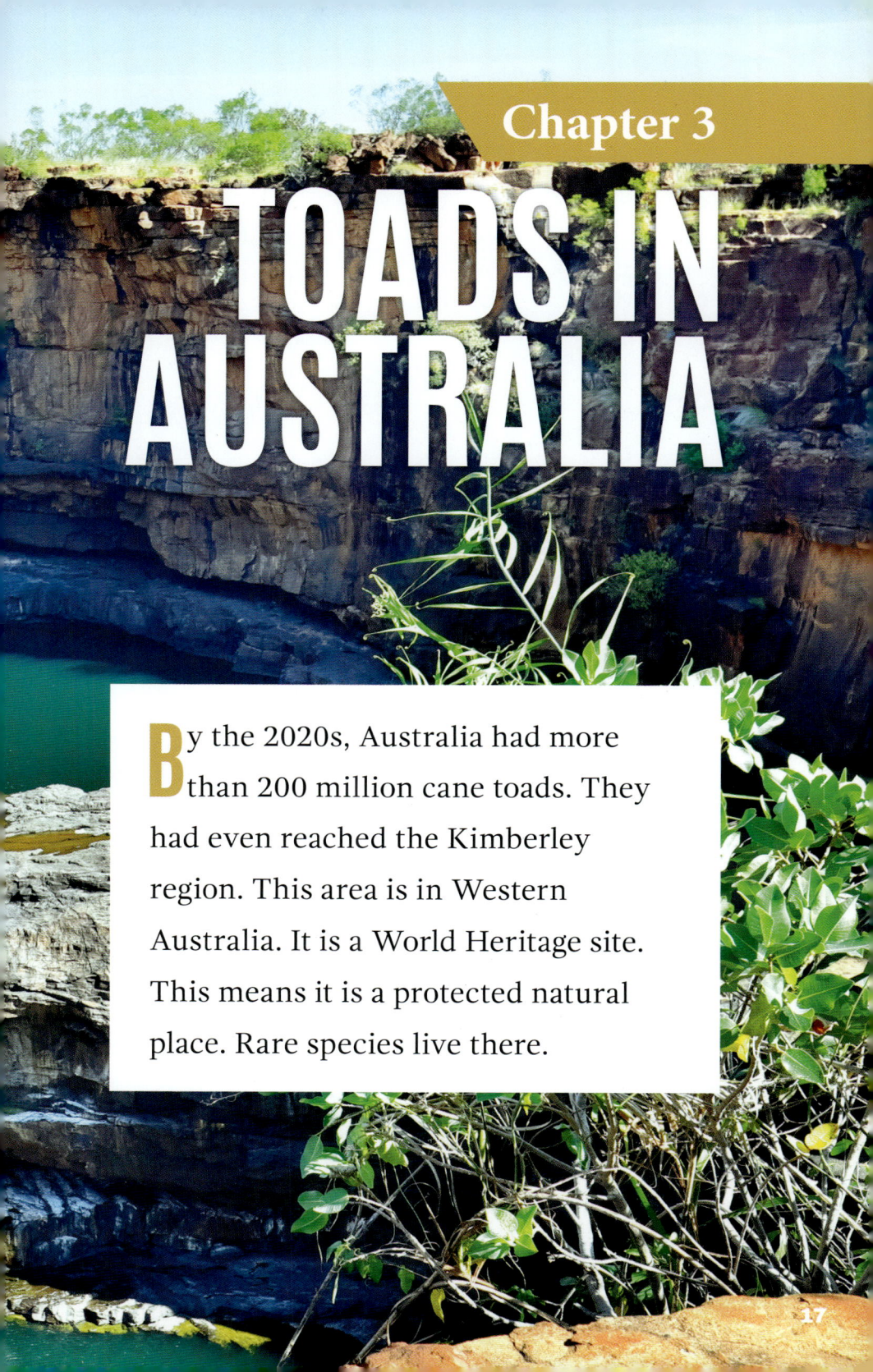

Chapter 3
TOADS IN AUSTRALIA

By the 2020s, Australia had more than 200 million cane toads. They had even reached the Kimberley region. This area is in Western Australia. It is a World Heritage site. This means it is a protected natural place. Rare species live there.

Cane toads spread across parts of Australia at a rate of more than 31 miles (50 km) each year.

Scientists were surprised to find cane toads in the Kimberley. Cane toads live in wet areas. The Kimberley tends to be dry. But it has a wet season. Scientists learned that the toads adapted. They traveled during the wet season. Then they stopped in the dry season. The toads found the small spots of water. They stayed there until the wet season returned.

Cane toads reached El Questro Wilderness Park in the Kimberley. After two years, there were hundreds of cane toads there. This place was home to quolls. The quoll is a rare type of marsupial. Quolls started eating the toads. The poison killed them. Soon, all the quolls in the area died.

FAST ADAPTERS

Animals have many ways of adapting to new areas. Even their bodies can change. In the 1930s, cane toads in Australia had short legs. But toads born later had longer legs. Those toads could move faster.

In some parts of Australia, groups of quolls have died out already.

Cane toads have also killed other predators in Australia. For example, freshwater crocodiles live only along Australian rivers. The Victoria River is one of them. When cane toads arrived there, crocodiles ate the toads and died. Scientists found 34 dead crocodiles at one spot.

TOADZILLA

In 2023, park rangers in Queensland found a huge toad. It weighed more than 5.5 pounds (2.5 kg). The rangers called it "Toadzilla." At the time, it was the largest cane toad ever found.

The park rangers gave "Toadzilla" to a museum. Scientists planned to study the toad's body.

23

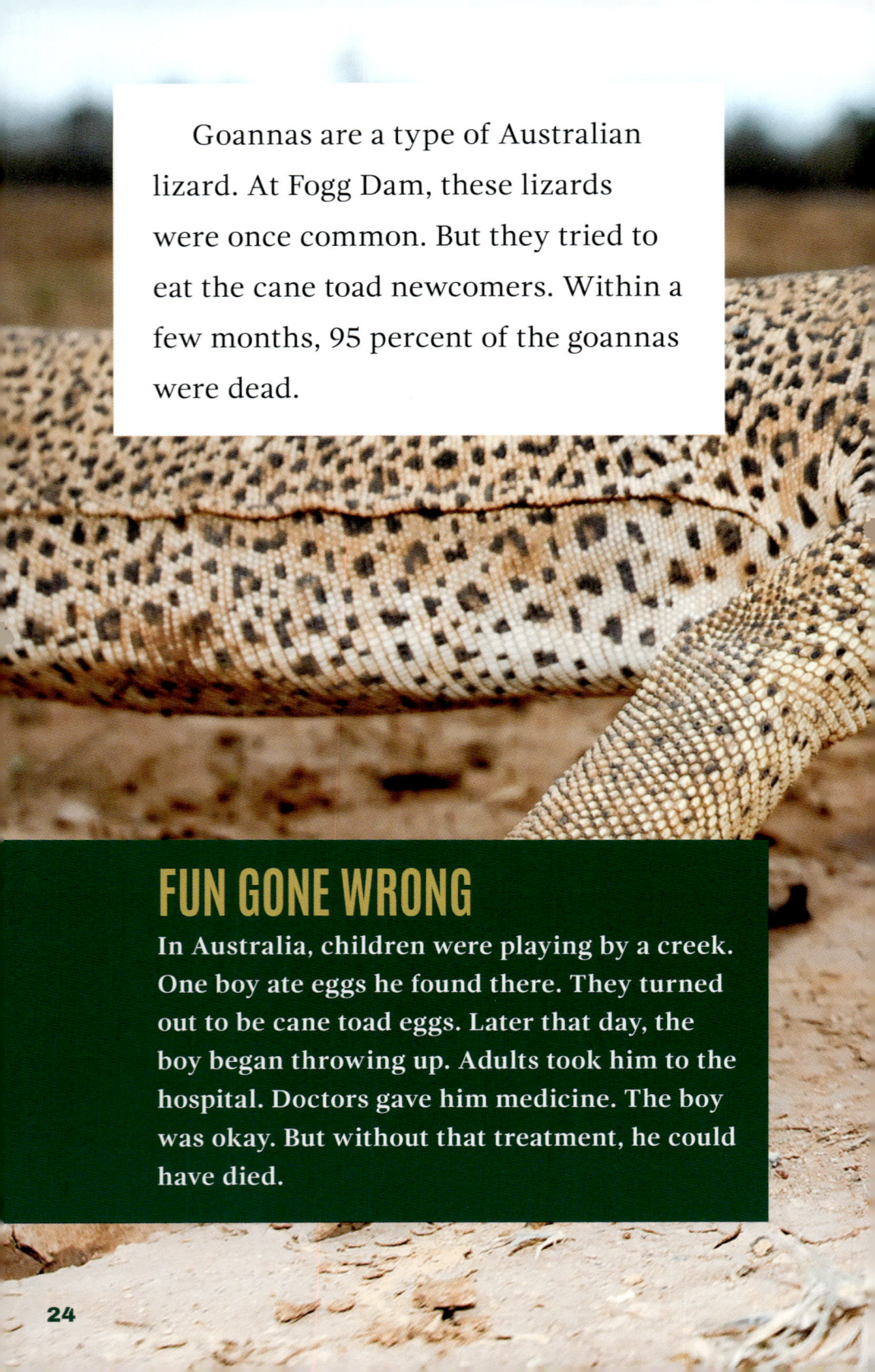

Goannas are a type of Australian lizard. At Fogg Dam, these lizards were once common. But they tried to eat the cane toad newcomers. Within a few months, 95 percent of the goannas were dead.

FUN GONE WRONG

In Australia, children were playing by a creek. One boy ate eggs he found there. They turned out to be cane toad eggs. Later that day, the boy began throwing up. Adults took him to the hospital. Doctors gave him medicine. The boy was okay. But without that treatment, he could have died.

Some yellow-spotted goannas grow more than 6 feet (2 m) long.

That's Wild!

CLOSE CALL

In the 2000s, New Zealand was free of cane toads. But one hiker almost changed that. She traveled from Australia to New Zealand. A cane toad hid in one of her boots. The woman went to a hiking store. She brought her boots in a canvas bag. The toad jumped out. Everyone was shocked. Workers at the store caught the toad. They put it in a freezer to kill it. Then the store gave the dead toad to the government.

Two other cane toad travelers almost entered New Zealand. Airport workers discovered one in someone's luggage. Another toad caught a ride in a crate from Fiji.

Toads may hide in shoes and luggage. People should check when traveling from places that have toads.

27

Chapter 4

TOADS IN FLORIDA

Cane toads have also caused many problems in Florida. The state's warm, wet climate makes it a great habitat. Toads live and breed in canals, swamps, streams, and ponds. They can even live in ditches and swimming pools.

Cane toads mainly live in the central and southern parts of Florida. But they are spreading around the state.

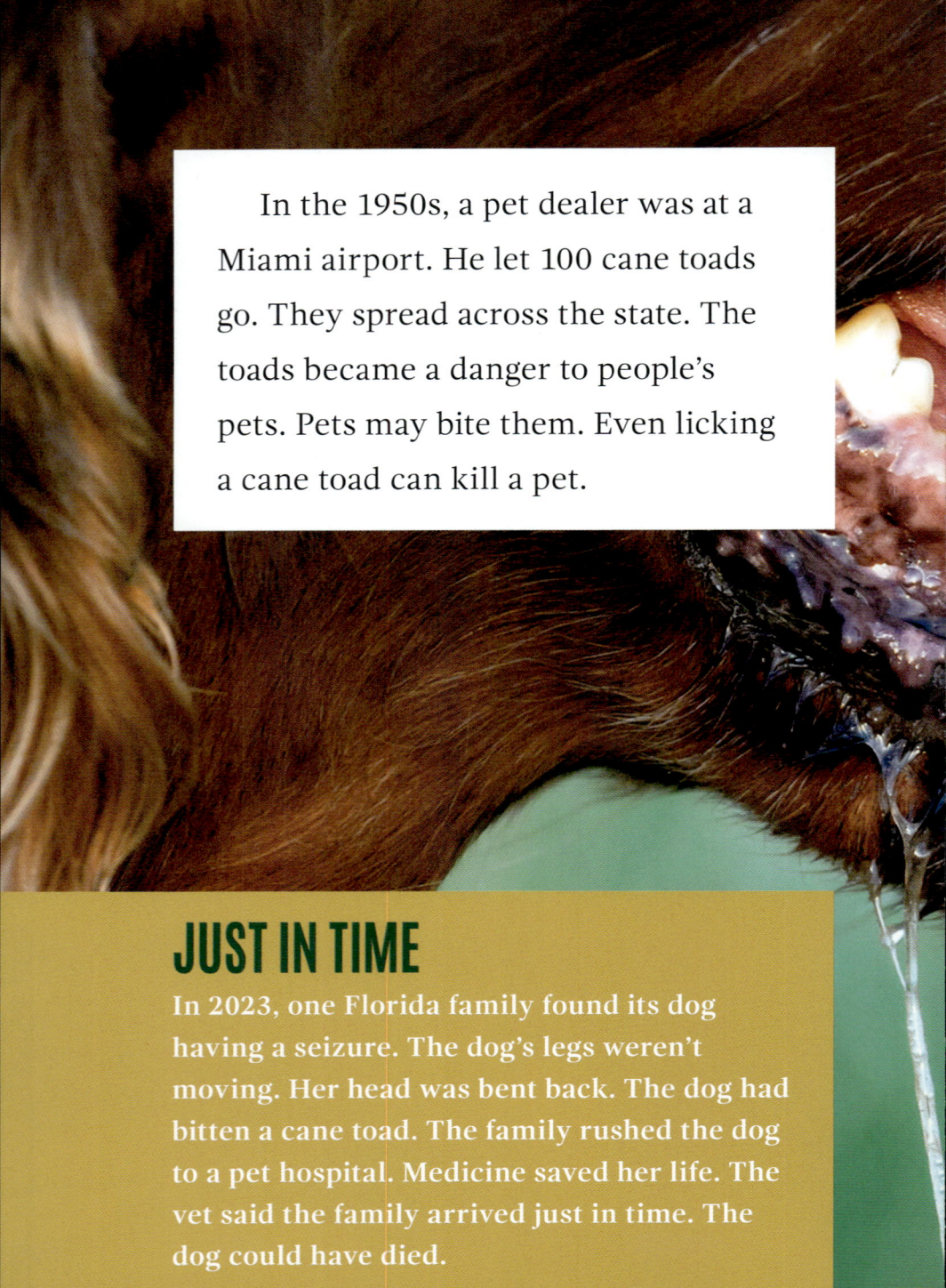

In the 1950s, a pet dealer was at a Miami airport. He let 100 cane toads go. They spread across the state. The toads became a danger to people's pets. Pets may bite them. Even licking a cane toad can kill a pet.

JUST IN TIME

In 2023, one Florida family found its dog having a seizure. The dog's legs weren't moving. Her head was bent back. The dog had bitten a cane toad. The family rushed the dog to a pet hospital. Medicine saved her life. The vet said the family arrived just in time. The dog could have died.

Pets drool and foam at the mouth after swallowing cane toad poison.

Southern toads only grow up to 4 inches (10 cm) long.

Cane toads are a threat to Florida's native animals. One is the southern toad. It eats the same things as cane toads. As a result, many southern toads don't have enough food. This can cause southern toad numbers to drop.

LOOKALIKES

Southern toads look similar to cane toads. Many people confuse them. But southern toads are smaller than cane toads. They have ridges on their heads. Cane toads do not. Southern toads also have oval glands. The glands of cane toads are shaped like triangles.

Cane toads can also get very noisy. A deep sound rolls from their throats. The sound is loud. And it's nonstop. Some people in Florida can't sleep as a result. One man took action. He bought a set of tongs. He put on a headlamp. Then the man went to nearby ponds. He caught all the toads he could. In one hour, he caught 68.

Toads have vocal sacs in their mouths. The sacs grow bigger when toads make noise.

Bugs often fly to lights. Then cane toads find and eat those bugs. Many people in Florida turn off outdoor lights at night. That helps keep cane toads away. People also try not to leave pet food or water bowls outside. They trim shrubs. They cut their grass short. People also get rid of clutter. These steps remove hiding places for toads.

WARM WINTER, MORE TOADS

Winters in Florida usually get too cold for cane toads. Many don't survive. But in 2022, the winter was warmer. That year, more cane toads made it to spring. This made them stronger. Their populations grew.

Short grass makes cane toads easier to find and catch.

37

That's Wild!

THE TOAD BUSINESS

In 2015, Jeannine Tilford started a company in Florida. She called it Toad Busters. The company helps people deal with cane toads. Workers find and catch toads near homes. The company started when Tilford found cane toads in her pool. One night, she put on goggles. She wore plastic bags on her hands. These protected her from toxins. She caught 130 toads in her pool.

Jeannine Tilford was a science teacher before she started Toad Busters.

39

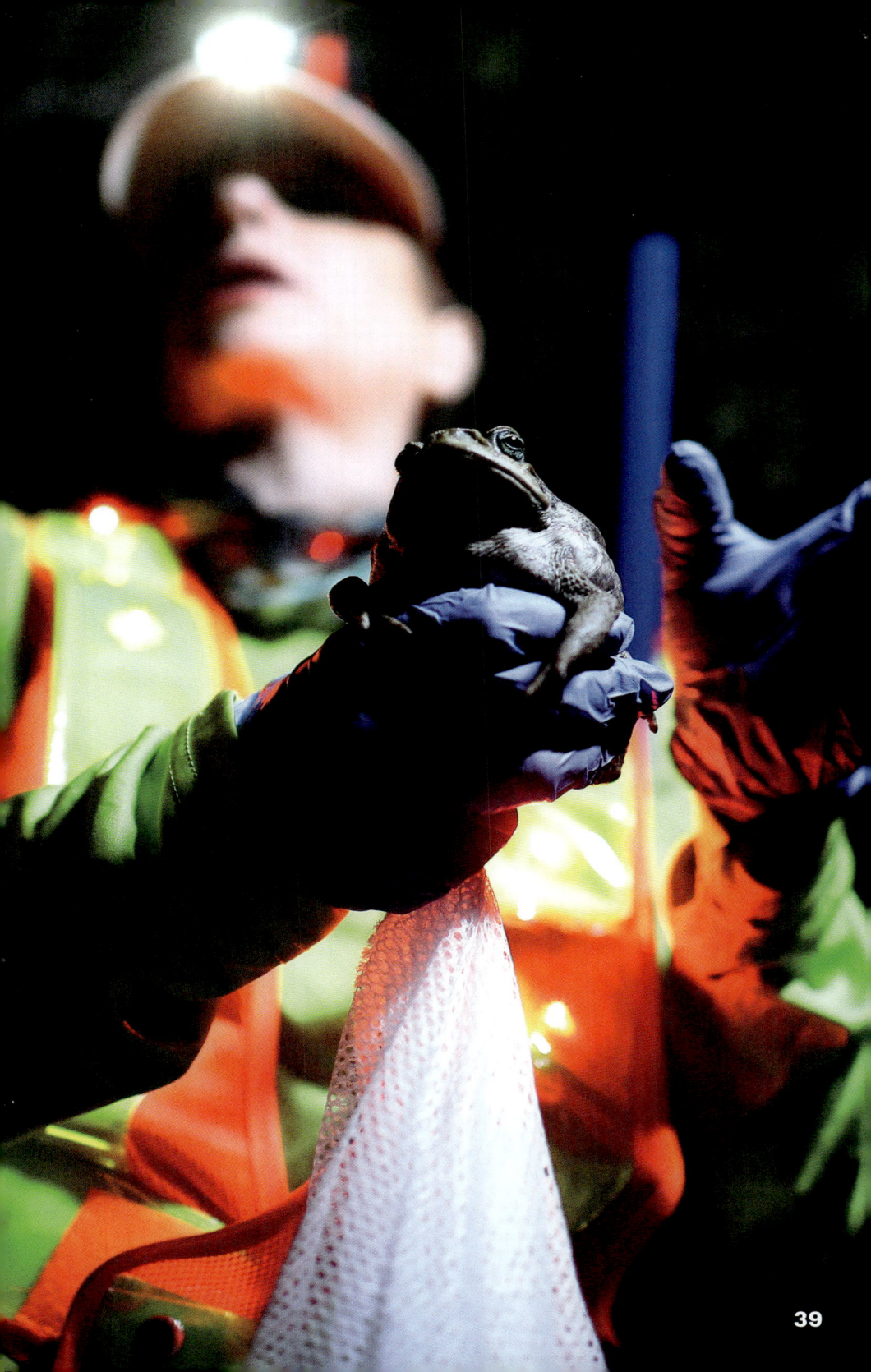

Chapter 5
AROUND THE WORLD

Cane toads have been introduced to more than 100 countries. Many of them are in the Pacific Ocean. For instance, the Philippines is made up of thousands of islands. Cane toads can be found on nearly all of them.

Few scientists have researched how cane toads have impacted the islands of the Philippines.

In 2019, mosquitoes were spreading disease in the Philippines. So, some local governments released cane toads. They hoped the toads would eat the mosquitoes. Scientists warned against this. They worried the toads would disrupt wildlife.

People found cane toads at Camp Kinser, a US military base in Japan.

TOAD VS. SOLDIER

In 2011, people spotted cane toads on a US base in Japan. No one had seen them on that island before. Workers, soldiers, and scientists all helped. They caught nearly 600 cane toads.

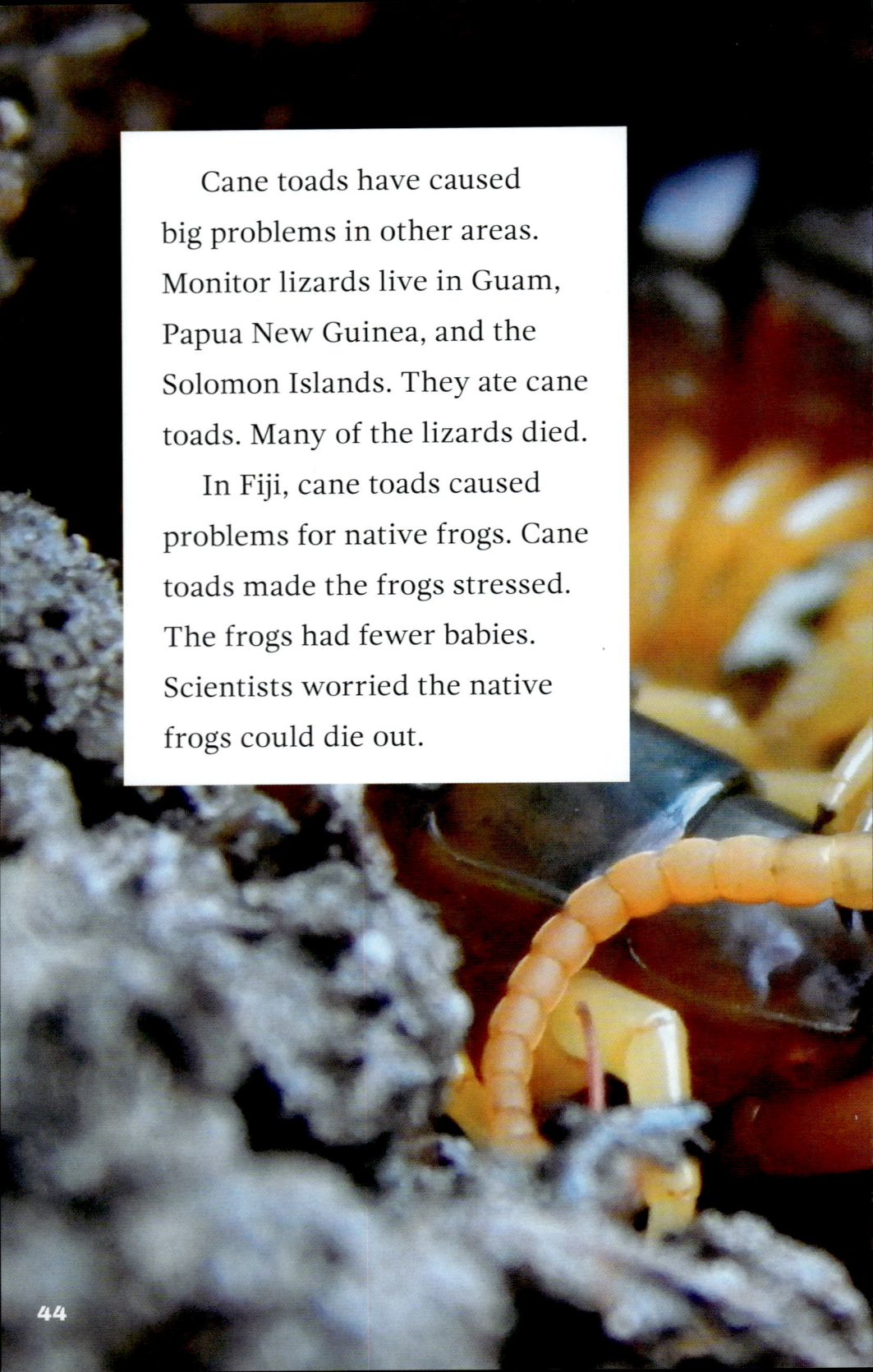

Cane toads have caused big problems in other areas. Monitor lizards live in Guam, Papua New Guinea, and the Solomon Islands. They ate cane toads. Many of the lizards died.

In Fiji, cane toads caused problems for native frogs. Cane toads made the frogs stressed. The frogs had fewer babies. Scientists worried the native frogs could die out.

Giant centipedes live on the Solomon Islands. These centipedes have died from trying to eat cane toads.

A girl looks at cane toads that were captured in Taiwan in 2021.

In 2021, people found cane toads in Taiwan. The toads were in a small town. Volunteers sprang into action. They caught every cane toad they could find. That way, the toads wouldn't spread.

HITCHHIKERS

Cane toads can be hitchhikers. They'll jump onto cars, trucks, and other vehicles. They often hide in soil that's being transported. Then the toads are carried to other areas. A new population starts.

The Caribbean is another area filled with cane toads. People brought toads to the region in the 1800s. Native predators died after eating the toads. One example is the Jamaican boa. This snake is the largest predator in Jamaica. Scientists found boas that died after eating cane toads.

THE BAHAMAS
In the 2000s, people in The Bahamas started spotting cane toads. The sightings raised alarm. The country's leaders started a task force. People found and killed the toads. But people found more toads in 2023. The country worked to get them back under control.

Jamaican boas are only found in Jamaica. If they die from eating cane toads, the snakes may go extinct.

Chapter 6
MANAGING CANE TOADS

When cane toads first arrive in a place, people can act fast. At first, there may be a few toads. It's still possible to catch and remove them. However, cane toads reproduce quickly. Soon, there are too many for people to catch. Then they can only be controlled.

Catching cane toads quickly is important. Cane toads may lay up to 30,000 eggs at one time.

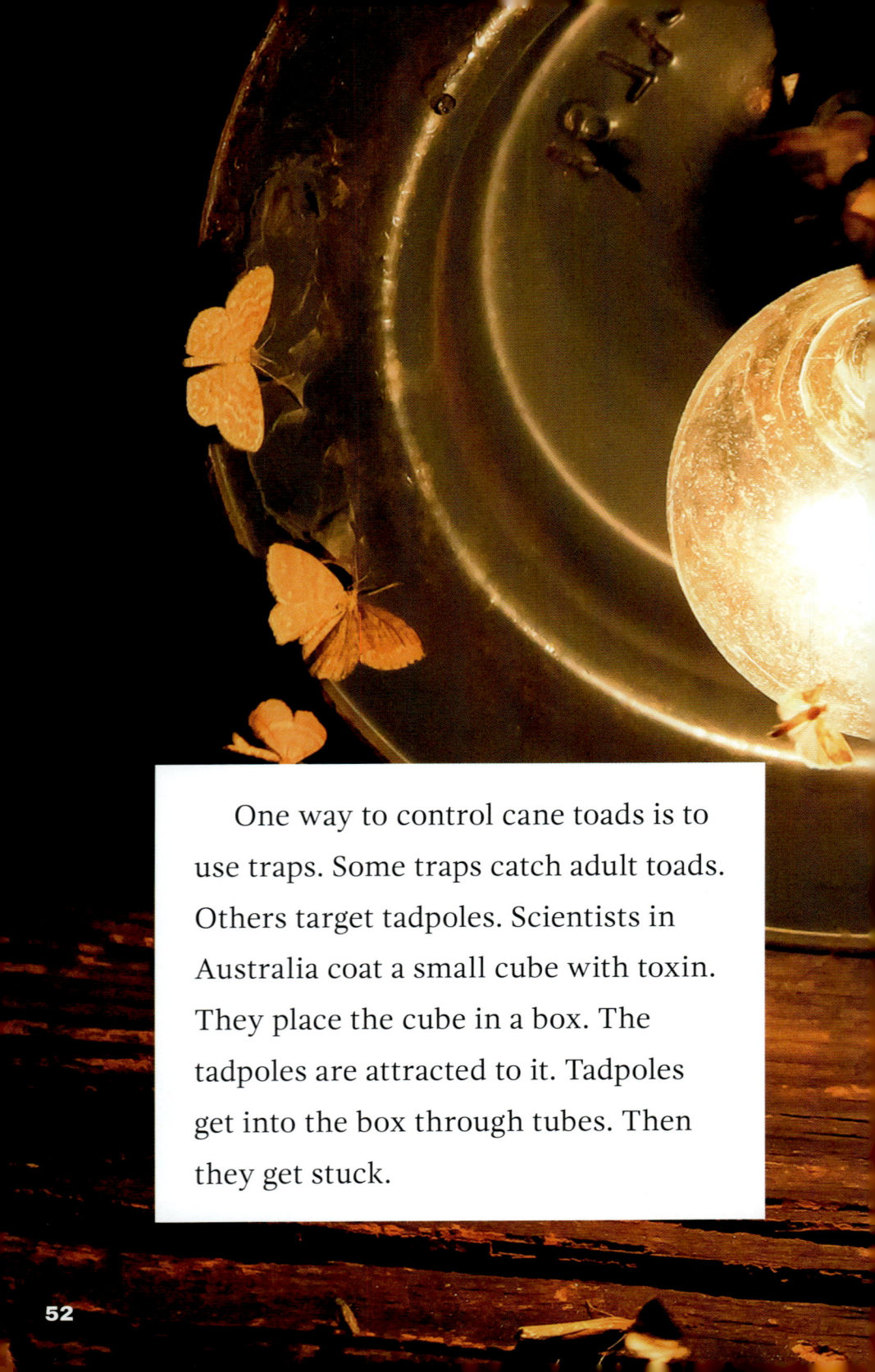

One way to control cane toads is to use traps. Some traps catch adult toads. Others target tadpoles. Scientists in Australia coat a small cube with toxin. They place the cube in a box. The tadpoles are attracted to it. Tadpoles get into the box through tubes. Then they get stuck.

Some traps use lights. Insects are drawn to the lights. Cane toads follow the bugs into traps.

PAINLESS DEATH

People often kill the cane toads they catch. But they don't want to cause pain. So, they place the toads in a fridge. The toads go into a deep sleep. After a day, people freeze the toads. But the toads don't feel anything.

People can also set up barriers. Cane toads can't hop very high. So, people put up fences and screens. Then toads can't reach certain areas. Cane toads can't live without water. For this reason, people often block off wet areas. They block off pools, dams, or ponds.

TREATING PETS

If a pet bites a cane toad, people can help. Adult owners can tip the pet's head down. They can wipe out their pet's mouth with a wet rag. They can also spray its mouth with a hose. Owners should rinse their pet's eyes. Then they can take it to the vet.

Cane toads cannot survive long without water. Fences help dry toads out.

Some scientists work to protect native animals. They teach them to avoid cane toads. For example, some scientists focused on goannas. They fed small toads to the goannas. The small toads have less poison. The goannas got sick. But they didn't die. They learned to not eat cane toads. This was passed on to their babies.

In places like Australia, scientists work to help native animals live alongside cane toads.

TOAD SAUSAGE

Some scientists made sausages out of cane toads. They fed the sausages to native animals. The sausages still tasted like the toads. But they had less poison. Animals that ate them got sick. They learned to stay away from cane toads.

MAP

① **Florida, United States:** People hire the Toad Busters company to catch cane toads in their yards.

② **Saint Catherine, Jamaica:** A Jamaican boa is found dead after eating a cane toad.

③ **Western Australia, Australia:** Cane toads invade the World Heritage site of the Kimberley.

4. **Okinawa, Japan:** People catch hundreds of cane toads after they are found on the island for the first time.

5. **Northern Territory, Australia:** Most goannas die at Fogg Dam when cane toads arrive.

6. **Queensland, Australia:** Volunteers catch tens of thousands of cane toads in the Great Cane Toad Bust.

7. **Viwa, Fiji:** Cane toads stress out Fijian ground frogs.

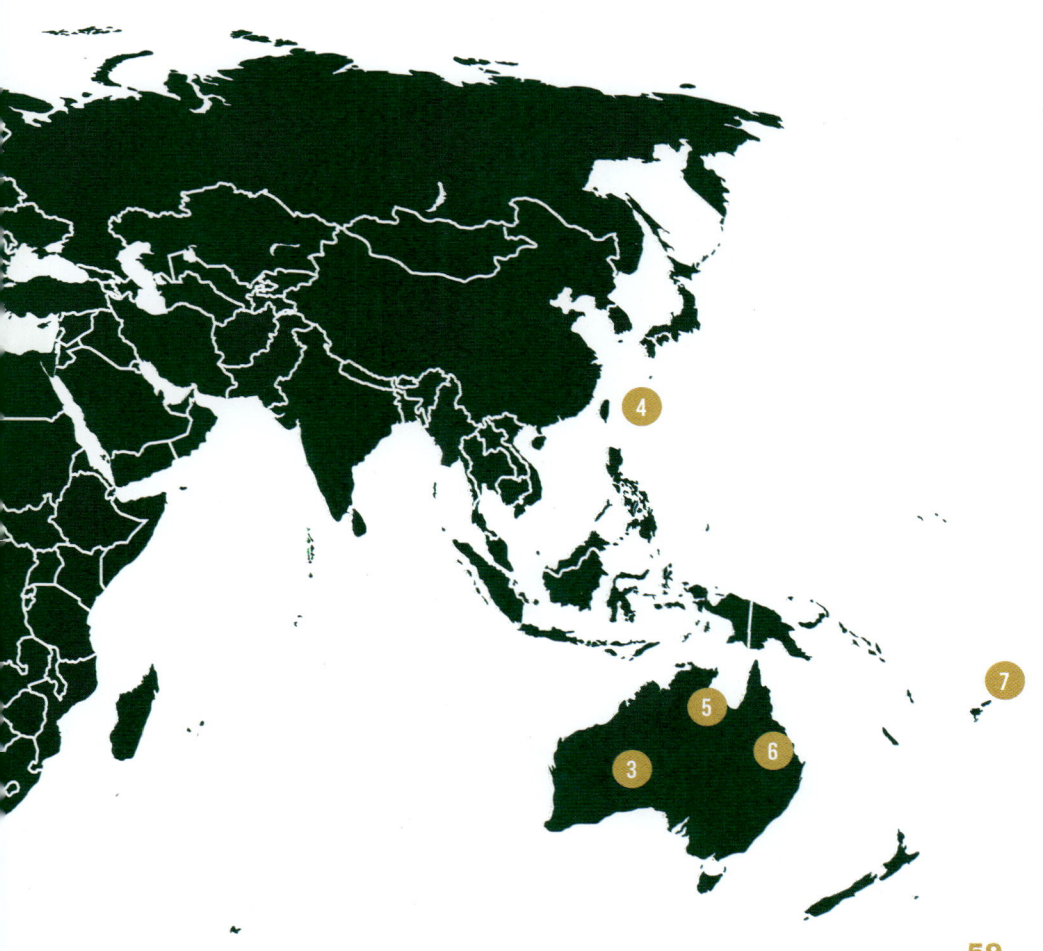

COMPREHENSION QUESTIONS

Write your answers on a separate piece of paper.

1. Write a paragraph explaining three ways that cane toads can harm native animals.

2. What do you think is the best way to control cane toads? Why?

3. When did people first bring cane toads to Australia?

    A. 1800s
    B. 1930s
    C. 2020s

4. How do cane toads kill predators?

    A. The toads' poison kills the predators after the toads are eaten.
    B. The toads eat the predators.
    C. The toads lead predators to larger animals.

5. What does **habitat** mean in this book?

*The state's warm, wet climate makes it a great **habitat**. Toads live and breed in canals, swamps, streams, and ponds.*

- A. a place to live
- B. a source of food
- C. a way to survive

6. What does **barriers** mean in this book?

*People can also set up **barriers**. Cane toads can't hop very high. So, people put up fences and screens.*

- A. wide-open paths
- B. very wet areas
- C. things that block the way

Answer key on page 64.

GLOSSARY

colonists
People who move to another area and take control.

glands
Body parts that release something, such as oils, tears, poison, or spit.

invasive
Spreading quickly in a new area and causing many problems there.

marsupial
A type of mammal that often has a pouch for its young.

native
Originally living in an area.

population
A group of animals living in a certain area.

predators
Animals that hunt and eat other animals.

species
A group of animals or plants that are similar and can breed with one another.

toxic
Harmful or poisonous.

TO LEARN MORE

BOOKS

Gilles, Renae. *Invasive Species in Infographics*. Ann Arbor, MI: Cherry Lake Publishing, 2021.

London, Martha. *Cane Toads*. Mendota Heights, MN: Focus Readers, 2022.

Wilcox, Merrie-Ellen. *Nature Out of Balance: How Invasive Species Are Changing the Planet*. Custer, WA: Orca Book Publishers, 2021.

ONLINE RESOURCES

Visit **www.apexeditions.com** to find links and resources related to this title.

ABOUT THE AUTHOR

Susan Rose Simms is a freelance writer and former speech and language pathologist. She writes children's books and educational materials. Her board book, *Let's Take a Trip*, was published by YES! Entertainment and won a Parents' Choice Award.

INDEX

Australia, 4, 6, 14, 17–24, 26, 52

Bahamas, The, 48

cane toad eggs, 11, 24
Caribbean, 12, 48
Central America, 12

Fiji, 26, 44
Florida, 28–36, 38
freshwater crocodiles, 22

goannas, 24, 56
Guam, 44

Hawai'i, 14

Jamaica, 48
Jamaican Boa, 48
Japan, 43

Kimberley, 17, 19–20

New Zealand, 26

Pacific, 40
Papua New Guinea, 44
pets, 30, 36, 54
Philippines, 40, 42

quolls, 20

Solomon Islands, 44
South America, 12
southern toads, 33
sugarcane, 12

tadpoles, 11, 52
Taiwan, 47
Tilford, Jeannine, 38
toad busting, 4, 6
Toadzilla, 22

Western Australia, 17

ANSWER KEY:
1. Answers will vary; 2. Answers will vary; 3. B; 4. A; 5. A; 6. C